INTO THE ETHER:

AN INVESTIGATIVE GUIDE TO PARANORMAL PHENOMENA

Dr. Rahul Joshi

Certified Professional Paranormal Investigator
6 Years' experience in the Paranormal field Investigation

TANEESHA
PUBLISHING

ISBN : 9788199146792
Edition : First, October 2025
Title : Into the Ether : An Investigative Guide to Paranormal Phenomena
Author : Dr. Rahul Joshi

Published by

TANEESHA PUBLISHING

An Imprint of **Taneesha and Prachi NextGen Publication**

Registered Office: Sunil Complex, 2nd Floor, Vijay Nagar,
Western Kutchery Road, Meerut - 250002, Uttar Pradesh, India
Website : www.taneeshapublishing.com
E-mail : help@taneeshapublishing.com
Phone : 91 8454812712

Printed by :
Manipal Technologies Limited, Bengaluru - 560001, Karnataka

Preface

The unknown has always fascinated humankind. For centuries, whispers of apparitions, unexplained phenomena, and other worldly encounters have permeated cultures across the globe. While mainstream science has often dismissed such accounts as folklore, psychological anomalies, or misinterpretations of natural events, there remains a compelling body of anecdotal and circumstantial evidence that warrants systematic exploration.

This book as a structured and scholarly introduction to the field of paranormal investigations. It seeks to bridge the gap between skepticism and belief by applying methodological rigor to phenomena that defy conventional explanation. Rather than attempting to prove or disprove the existence of the paranormal, the purpose of this work is to explore how such phenomena are studied, documented, and interpreted in contemporary investigative practice.

Drawing from case studies, historical accounts, field research techniques, and emerging technologies, this book is designed for both aspiring investigators and curious readers seeking a grounded understanding of the subject. Emphasis is placed on critical thinking, ethical inquiry, and scientific integrity—principles that are essential when navigating the often-murky waters of the unknown.

I invite the readers, to approach this text with an open yet discerning mind. Whether you are a skeptic, a believer, or a cautious inquirer, may these pages challenge your assumptions, enrich your understanding, and perhaps even inspire you to embark on your own search beyond the veil.

Dr. Rahul Joshi
Certified Professional Paranormal Investigator
October 2025

Acknowledgment

The journey of writing this book has been as enlightening as it has been challenging. It would not have been possible without the support, guidance, and encouragement of many individuals and institutions, all of whom I wish to acknowledge with deep appreciation.

First and foremost, I extend my sincere gratitude to the researchers, investigators, and scholars—both past and present—whose work laid the foundation for this exploration into the unknown. Their courage to question reality and document the inexplicable has been an inspiration.

To my colleagues and peers in the field of paranormal studies and metaphysical research, thank you for your insightful discussions, critical feedback, and the shared passion for understanding what lies beyond the ordinary.

I am especially grateful to the individuals and families who opened their homes, shared their experiences, and trusted me with their stories. Your willingness to speak about the inexplicable with honesty and vulnerability added invaluable depth to this work.

Finally, to the countless readers, investigators, and seekers around the world—this book was written with you in mind. May it serve as a compass as you explore the boundaries of perception, belief, and reality.

Dr. Rahul Joshi
Certified Professional Paranormal Investigator
October 2025

RB

Contents

	Building and Outreach # Sustaining Team Morale and Cohesion # Funding your Team # Team Structure with Responsibility # Conclusion # Sample Client Intake Form.	

Chapter One

An Introduction: Beyond the Normal

1.1 What is "Paranormal"?

The term paranormal encompasses phenomena that exist or occur outside the bounds of scientific explanation. Derived from the Greek prefix para- meaning "beside" or "beyond," and normalis, from Latin, referring to conformity or rule, the paranormal refers to events or experiences that fall outside the scope of normal scientific understanding. It does not necessarily imply the supernatural, but rather designates areas that are presently unexplained by conventional science (Irwin & Watt, 2007).

Paranormal investigations involve exploring and examining claims of paranormal activity, such as ghosts, hauntings, UFOs, and other unexplained phenomena, using a combination of scientific methods, equipment, and techniques.

Paranormal phenomena are typically identified through anecdotal evidence—unverified experiences reported by individuals. Such phenomena include hauntings, apparitions, poltergeist activity, extrasensory perception (ESP), telekinesis, and unidentified aerial phenomena (UAPs). While these experiences are often highly subjective, their persistence across cultures and historical epochs suggests an enduring psychological and cultural significance.

1.2 Natural, Supernatural, and Paranormal: Clarifying Definitions

To conduct a rigorous investigation into claims of paranormal activity, it is essential to distinguish between terms often used interchangeably:

- **Natural phenomena:** Observable occurrences governed by physical laws (e.g., weather patterns, gravitational forces).
- **Supernatural phenomena:** Believed to be caused by forces or entities beyond nature or physical laws, often tied to religious or mythological systems (e.g., divine intervention, spirits).
- **Paranormal phenomena:** Occurrences that appear to defy

scientific explanation, but which may—at least in theory—be subject to eventual understanding through empirical inquiry.

The paranormal exists in a conceptual liminal space—neither fully accepted nor wholly dismissed by scientific orthodoxy. While skeptics argue that all phenomena must eventually submit to scientific scrutiny or be discarded, proponents argue that science must expand its parameters to account for anomalous data (Braude, 1997).

1.3 Why Do People Report Paranormal Experiences?

Human perception is inherently fallible, and cognitive psychology has demonstrated that a wide range of experiences—such as sleep paralysis, hallucinations, infrasound exposure, and misinterpretation of environmental stimuli—can contribute to perceived paranormal events (French & Stone, 2014). Nevertheless, the universality of these reports across cultures and eras suggests that the paranormal cannot be wholly reduced to misperception.

Several theories attempt to explain the prevalence of paranormal belief:

- **Psychological explanations:** Include pattern recognition (pareidolia), suggestibility, confirmation bias, and cognitive dissonance reduction.
- **Sociocultural factors:** Social reinforcement, cultural narratives, and religious traditions can shape the interpretation of anomalous experiences.
- **Neurological theories:** Suggest that temporal lobe anomalies, particularly micro-seizures, may contribute to intense feelings of presence or visions (Persinger, 1987).
- **Environmental variables:** Cold spots, electromagnetic field fluctuations, or infrasound may lead to sensations or interpretations aligned with paranormal reports.

Understanding the cognitive and environmental contexts behind these experiences is foundational to designing investigations that aim to discern between natural causes and truly unexplained phenomena.

1.4 Categories of Paranormal Phenomena

Scholars and investigators typically classify paranormal events into distinct, though often overlapping, categories. Below is a non-exhaustive typology:

a) Apparitions and Hauntings

Visual manifestations of persons (living or dead) with no physical source. Hauntings are often categorized as either residual (repetitive, environmental imprints) or intelligent (interactions implying consciousness).

b) Poltergeist Activity

Characterized by disruptive physical phenomena—such as objects moving or breaking, unexplained noises, or spontaneous fires. These cases often center around adolescent individuals and may reflect psychosomatic or psychological conditions.

c) Extrasensory Perception (ESP)

Includes telepathy, clairvoyance, precognition, and remote viewing. Though widely researched by parapsychologists, consistent empirical support remains elusive (Bem & Honorton, 1994).

d) Psychokinesis (PK)

The purported ability to move or influence objects with the mind. Laboratory research into micro-PK (e.g., random number generator influence) has yielded controversial results.

e) Cryptids and Unidentified Beings

Claims of creatures such as Bigfoot, Mokele-mbembe, or the Loch Ness Monster fall under cryptozoology—a subset of paranormal investigation tied closely to folklore and biology.

f) UFOs and UAPs

Unidentified aerial (or anomalous) phenomena are currently under renewed investigation by government and scientific agencies. While some reports suggest technological anomalies, others imply psychological misinterpretation or sociocultural artifacts.

1.5 Scientific Skepticism and the Role of Critical Thinking

Scientific skepticism does not imply cynicism but emphasizes methodical doubt and the requirement of robust evidence. Paranormal investigators, whether affiliated with institutions or working independently, must employ critical thinking to navigate between open-minded inquiry and the dangers of confirmation bias.

Key principles of critical inquiry in paranormal research include:

- **Falsifiability:** Claims should be testable and capable of being disproven.
- **Replication:** Phenomena should be reproducible under controlled conditions.
- **Peer Review and Transparency:** Investigations should document methodology and submit findings to scrutiny.
- **Occam's Razor:** When presented with competing explanations, the simplest adequate one should be preferred.

1.6 Objectives of Paranormal Investigations:

1. **Data collection:** Gather evidence and data to support or debunk paranormal claims.
2. **Explanation:** Provide logical explanations for reported phenomena, if possible.
3. **Understanding:** Shed light on the nature of paranormal activity, if it exists.

1.7 Key aspects of Paranormal Investigations:

1. **Equipment:** Utilize various tools, such as EMF meters, infrared cameras, digital recorders, and more.
2. **Investigation protocols:** Establish systematic approaches to ensure thorough coverage and minimize false positives.
3. **Data analysis:** Examine collected data, audio, video, and photographs for anomalies.
4. **Debunking:** Rule out natural causes for reported phenomena.
5. **Spirit communication:** Attempt to communicate with entities, if applicable.

6. **Client support:** Provide guidance and assistance to clients experiencing paranormal activity.

1.8 Types of investigations:

- **Residential:** Investigating private homes and apartments.
- **Commercial:** Examining businesses, hotels, and public establishments.
- **Historical:** Investigating allegedly haunted historical sites and landmarks.
- **Outdoor:** Exploring paranormal activity in outdoor environments, such as forests or fields.

1.9 Challenges in Investigation:

- **False positives:** Misinterpreting natural phenomena as paranormal.
- **Hoaxes:** Dealing with intentionally fabricated claims.
- **Equipment limitations:** Recognizing the constraints of investigation equipment.
- **Client expectations:** Managing client hopes and fears.

1.10 Importance of Scientific Approach in Paranormal Investigations

The scientific approach is crucial in paranormal investigations for several reasons:

Science and Paranormal which believes in using the proven facts proved the unknown e.g the first EVP was recorded by Thomas Edison who was a scientist & inventor of light bulb. Same is the case with G. Bell inventor of telephone had EVPs of her dead mother. Mostly rationalists have closed minds.

1. **Objectivity:** A scientific approach helps investigators remain objective and unbiased, reducing the influence of personal beliefs and emotions.
2. **Systematic methodology:** It ensures a systematic and structured investigation, covering all aspects and minimizing false positives.

3. **Data collection and analysis:** Scientific methods enable thorough data collection and analysis, helping to identify patterns and anomalies.
4. **Debunking:** A scientific approach helps rule out natural explanations for reported phenomena, increasing the credibility of potential paranormal findings.
5. **Credibility:** Employing scientific methods enhances the credibility of investigations and findings, making them more acceptable to the scientific community.
6. **Replicability:** Scientific investigations aim for replicability, allowing others to verify findings and build upon existing research.
7. **Minimizing Misinterpretation:** A scientific approach reduces the risk of misinterpreting natural phenomena as paranormal.
8. **Advancing knowledge:** By applying scientific methods, investigators can contribute to the advancement of knowledge in the field of paranormal research.

1.11 Importance of Spiritual Approach in Paranormal Investigations

Religion and Paranormal which believes in existence of spirits. Every holy book has something mentioned about the spirits and how to tackle them. The approach in every religion is different but the common thing is belief system. In many religion regard ghosts and spirits as demon, fallen angels and things to stay away from like Ouija Board, Psychics, medium, dowsing rods & etc.

1. **Protection Rituals:** Perform protection rituals, such as smudging or prayer, to safeguard investigators and clients.
2. **Spiritual Grounding:** Encourage investigators to ground themselves spiritually, through meditation or prayer, to maintain a clear and focused mindset.
3. **Set Intentions:** Clearly define the investigation's intentions and goals, ensuring a focused and respectful approach.

1.12 Importance of Spiritual & Scientific (Blended) Approach in Paranormal Investigations

Blended Approach means a combination of Spiritual and Scientific approach. It means having faith on your beliefs use the scientific methods, tools and techniques and modern gadgets investigate the facts and analyzing the evidences and then draw any conclusion and go for finding a solution and implementing it for real life situation.

According to me the most preferable approach is Blended Approach because here we are not in the situation to look at the matter with single perspective one coin has two sides and if any one wishes to explore the history of that coin one should check thoroughly both the side of the coin. Likewise taking situation from spiritual and scientific side we get a broader horizon to think, analyze and act on it.

By embracing a scientific approach, paranormal investigators can increase the validity and reliability of their findings, ultimately helping to better understand the nature of paranormal phenomena.

1.13 Conclusion:

An academic approach to paranormal investigation does not require belief in the phenomena under study, but it demands a commitment to rigor, documentation, and intellectual humility. The goal is not to prove or disprove the existence of the paranormal, but to understand it through structured inquiry.

Chapter Two

Historical Foundations of Paranormal Investigation

2.1 Origins in Ancient Civilizations

Human curiosity about the unknown dates back to prehistoric times. Archaeological records indicate that early humans believed in spirits, gods, and other unseen forces influencing daily life. Burial rituals, shamanic practices, and cave paintings all suggest a rich spiritual cosmology where the line between the natural and supernatural was fluid.

- **Ancient Egypt:** The Egyptians believed in an afterlife and spiritual presence, as evidenced by funerary texts like the Book of the Dead. Temples and tombs were thought to be spiritually active spaces.
- **Mesopotamia:** Texts from the Akkadian and Sumerian periods describe demons (utukku) and ghosts (edimmu) who could haunt the living if burial rites were not observed.
- **India and East Asia:** Vedic literature contains references to disembodied souls (preta), while Chinese culture developed complex ghost beliefs influenced by Confucianism, Taoism, and Buddhism.
- **Classical Greece and Rome:** Philosophers like Plato and Plotinus considered the soul's immortality, and stories of spectral apparitions appear in early Roman literature, such as Pliny the Younger's account of a haunted house in Athens.

These traditions did not distinguish sharply between religion, philosophy, and what would today be considered paranormal phenomena. Instead, the spiritual world was a natural extension of daily existence.

2.2 The Rise of Mysticism and Religious Doctrine

During the medieval period, the interpretation of paranormal events was increasingly absorbed into religious worldviews. Christianity in Europe came to dominate interpretations of spiritual and anomalous activity, often labeling unexplained occurrences as demonic.

- **Saintly Miracles and Apparitions:** Catholic hagiographies described levitation, bilocation, incorruptible bodies, and divine visions.
- **Exorcism Practices:** The Rituale Romanum codified procedures for confronting demonic possession. While intended as spiritual acts, these rituals often resembled modern paranormal interventions.
- **Islamic Mysticism (Sufism):** Sufi literature recounts spiritual visions, communication with angels, and mystical states, and all considered part of divine proximity.

In contrast to modern skepticism, these experiences were interpreted through the dominant theological lens, and attempts to question or investigate them outside religious doctrine were often discouraged—or punished.

2.3 Early Scientific Inquiry and Enlightenment Thought

The Enlightenment (17th–18th century) emphasized rationality, empirical observation, and skepticism toward superstition. While this period advanced scientific understanding, it also saw renewed interest in the paranormal under the guise of natural philosophy and experimental curiosity.

- **Franz Mesmer (1734–1815):** Introduced "animal magnetism," a precursor to hypnotism, claiming invisible forces affected human behavior—an idea bridging science and mysticism.
- **Emanuel Swedenborg (1688–1772):** Described spiritual realms he claimed to explore through altered consciousness, merging theology with psychic perception.
- **Magnetic séances and automata:** In aristocratic circles, interest in mechanical marvels and spirit communication became fashionable, laying groundwork for later spiritualist practices.

The tension between belief and skepticism, faith and empiricism, created a fertile ground for early psychical speculation.

2.4 The Spiritualist Movement and the Birth of Psychical Research

The modern era of paranormal investigation began in earnest with the Spiritualist movement in the mid-19th century. Sparked by the famous Fox sisters of New York in 1848, who claimed to communicate with a ghost through rapping sounds, Spiritualism quickly gained traction in North America and Europe.

Features of the Movement:

- **Séances:** Mediums claimed to serve as conduits for spirits. Manifestations included rapping, automatic writing, ectoplasm, and spirit photography.
- **Popular Figures:** Daniel Dunglas Home, Eusapia Palladino, and Leonora Piper became famous mediums, performing under both public scrutiny and academic investigation.
- **Cultural Impact:** Spiritualist churches, publications, and gatherings proliferated, especially after the mass bereavement caused by the American Civil War and World War I.

This movement catalyzed both public interest and scholarly skepticism, leading to the emergence of formal investigative organizations.

Emergence of Psychical Research:

- The Society for Psychical Research (SPR), founded in London in 1882, sought to apply scientific methods to the study of telepathy, apparitions, and mediumship.
- Early members included philosopher Henry Sidgwick, physicist William Barrett, and psychologist Frederic W. H. Myers.
- The American Society for Psychical Research (ASPR) followed in 1885, involving scholars like William James.
- These organizations pioneered field investigations, case documentation, and attempts at laboratory replication.

2.5 Key Figures in Early Paranormal Investigation

Harry Price (1881–1948)

A British psychic researcher and investigator best known for his work on Borley Rectory, dubbed "the most haunted house in England." Price emphasized the use of technology (photography, telegraphs) and strict documentation in his investigations.

J. B. Rhine (1895–1980)

An American botanist turned parapsychologist who founded the Parapsychology Laboratory at Duke University. Rhine developed statistical methods for studying ESP and psychokinesis using Zener cards and random event generators, legitimizing laboratory-based study.

Eleanor Sidgwick (1845–1936)

Often overlooked, she contributed significantly to the SPR's research and methodology. Her work on case analysis set early standards for skeptical inquiry.

Hans Holzer (1920–2009)

One of the first popular paranormal investigators in the 20th century, Holzer combined academic study with public outreach, authoring over 100 books and coining terms still in use today.

These pioneers advanced both the methodology and public perception of paranormal research. Their work laid the foundation for contemporary field investigation and inspired future generations of ghost hunters, parapsychologists, and skeptics alike.

2.6 Paranormal Investigation in the 20th Century

The 20th century witnessed rapid developments in both technology and popular interest in the paranormal:

- **Spirit Photography and EVP:** Devices like reel-to-reel tape recorders were used to capture "spirit voices" (Electronic Voice Phenomena), first claimed by Friedrich Jürgenson in the 1950s.
- **Haunting Investigations:** The Enfield Poltergeist case (1977–1979) in England received extensive press coverage and scholarly debate. Investigators Maurice Grosse and Guy Lyon Playfair documented levitations, voices, and moving objects—while skeptics questioned their reliability.
- **Rise of Popular Media:** Films like The Exorcist (1973), Poltergeist (1982), and television series like Unsolved Mysteries shaped public imagination and spawned a wave of amateur investigators.

- **UFO Research and Government Interest:** Following the 1947 Roswell incident and Project Blue Book, interest in UFOs surged, culminating in declassified documents and modern UAP research programs.

This era also saw increased commercialization and entertainment-based approaches, occasionally undermining rigorous inquiry. Nonetheless, many serious researchers continued to promote academic approaches, such as using controlled experiments and interdisciplinary methods.

2.7 Transition to the Contemporary Era

Today, paranormal investigation spans a wide spectrum—from scientific parapsychology to folkloric anthropology, amateur ghost hunting, and media-based entertainment. Advances in digital technology (infrared cameras, EMF detectors, audio spectrum analysis) have democratized field investigation, allowing smaller teams to collect, document, and analyze data.

Simultaneously, academic interest has shifted toward the psychological and cultural significance of paranormal beliefs. Universities have hosted conferences on anomalistic psychology, and scholars such as Christopher French, Susan Blackmore, and David Luke continue to examine altered consciousness, belief formation, and perception anomalies.

The historical trajectory of paranormal investigation reveals a persistent human fascination with the unknown. From ancient rituals to modern electromagnetic field meters, the quest to understand anomalies has evolved alongside our scientific and cultural frameworks. While methodology and public attitudes have fluctuated, the core impulse—to investigate that which lies beyond conventional explanation—remains a consistent feature of human inquiry.

Chapter Three

Classifying Paranormal Phenomena

3.1 The Need for Classification in Paranormal Research

A key aspect of any systematic investigation is the ability to categorize observed or reported phenomena. In scientific disciplines, classification provides a common language for researchers and allows for the development of theoretical frameworks, methodological approaches, and comparative analysis. Similarly, in paranormal investigation, developing a typology of anomalous phenomena helps differentiate between various experiences and informs appropriate investigative strategies.

While the classification of paranormal phenomena is complicated by the subjective nature of reports and the absence of universally accepted mechanisms, a working typology has emerged from field research, psychical studies, and cross-cultural observation.

3.2 Residual vs. Intelligent Hauntings

a) Residual Hauntings

A residual haunting is understood as a non-interactive, recurring manifestation of past events. These are often described as "energy imprints"—a form of environmental memory in which a traumatic or emotionally charged event is believed to be imprinted onto a physical space.

Characteristics:

- Repetitive and predictable occurrences.
- No awareness or interaction with the observer.
- Often associated with historical events (e.g., battles, murders).
- May include visual, auditory, or olfactory components.

Theoretical Basis:

While speculative, theories suggest that high-energy events could produce a form of psychometric residue detectable under certain environmental conditions (Stone, 2004). However, no empirical mechanism has been validated.

b) Intelligent Hauntings

These involve manifestations that appear to exhibit awareness, intentionality, and interaction with human observers. Reports may include direct communication, responses to questions, or object manipulation.

Characteristics:

- Variable behavior in response to stimuli.
- Personal references or recognition of individuals.
- Apparent personality or memory continuity.

Implications:

Investigators often treat intelligent hauntings as potential evidence of consciousness survival. Such cases require detailed documentation, repeated observation, and careful analysis to eliminate psychological or environmental confounds.

3.3 Poltergeists

The term poltergeist originates from German, meaning "noisy ghost." Poltergeist activity involves spontaneous, often violent, physical disturbances such as object displacement, unexplained knocking sounds, furniture movement, and—in rare cases—bodily harm.

Distinguishing Features:

- Recurrent psychokinetic phenomena.
- Tends to cluster around a specific individual, often adolescents.
- Episodes escalate and then cease without intervention.
- May include electrical disturbances or spontaneous fires.

Psychological Interpretations:

Some researchers, including William Roll (1972), have suggested that poltergeist activity may be a form of recurrent spontaneous psychokinesis (RSPK)—a subconscious expression of repressed emotional conflict, particularly in youth.

Investigative Considerations:

Investigators must rule out fraud, mischief, and environmental factors. Controlled conditions, witness separation, and video documentation are essential for credible inquiry.

3.4 Shadow People and Apparitional Entities

Shadow people are described as humanoid silhouettes, often seen peripherally or during sleep paralysis. Unlike traditional ghosts, they are typically formless, fast-moving, and produce an atmosphere of dread.

Categories of Apparitional Entities:

- **Full-bodied apparitions:** Visually distinct, seemingly solid entities, often perceived as deceased individuals.
- **Partial apparitions:** Faces, limbs, or indistinct forms.
- **Phantom animals:** Reported sightings of non-living animals, often tied to folklore or local legend.
- **Interactive spirits:** Apparitions that appear responsive or communicative.

Scientific and Psychological Perspectives:

Shadow entities may arise from hypnagogic hallucinations, REM intrusion, or low-light visual anomalies. The amygdala's response to ambiguous stimuli may also account for fear reactions.

3.5 Orbs, Mists, and Light Anomalies

Orbs and luminous anomalies have gained popularity due to digital photography, where unexplained balls of light often appear in images taken at haunted locations.

Orbs:

- Spherical light artifacts, usually white, blue, or green.
- Commonly attributed to dust, insects, or lens flare.
- Advocates claim behavioral patterns or energy changes correlate with orb appearances.

Mists and Fog-Like Forms:

- Wispy shapes appearing in photographs or video.
- Hypotheses include breath condensation, smoke, or temperature inversions.
- Rarely observed by the naked eye, limiting their evidentiary value.

Analytical Techniques:

High-resolution cameras, particle analysis, and controlled shooting environments are recommended for evaluating visual anomalies.

3.6 Possession and Spirit Attachment

Spirit possession is a widely reported phenomenon, particularly within religious and anthropological contexts. It involves the belief that a non-corporeal entity inhabits or influences a living person.

Symptoms Commonly Reported:

- Personality shifts and altered voice patterns.
- Aversion to sacred symbols.
- Superhuman strength or glossolalia (speaking in unknown tongues).
- Memory loss or trance-like states.

Cross-Cultural Interpretations:

- **Catholicism:** Frames possession within the doctrine of demonic influence, addressed via exorcism.
- **Hinduism and Buddhism:** Allow for both benign and malevolent spirit influence.
- **West African and Afro-Caribbean traditions:** Often incorporate possession in ceremonial contexts as communion with deities.

Investigative Challenges:

Differentiating psychological illness (e.g., dissociative identity disorder, schizophrenia) from possession is critical. Collaboration with mental health professionals is advised before attributing causality to paranormal agents.

3.7 Extrasensory Perception (ESP) and Telepathy

ESP refers to the reception of information not conveyed through the recognized senses. Common subtypes include:

- **Telepathy:** Mind-to-mind communication.
- **Clairvoyance:** Knowledge of distant or hidden objects.
- **Precognition:** Foreknowledge of future events.
- **Retro-Cognition:** Awareness of past events outside normal memory.

Experimental Approaches:

- **Ganzfeld Experiments:** Attempt to detect telepathy under sensory deprivation conditions.

- **Remote Viewing:** Individuals attempt to describe distant locations with no prior exposure.
- **Zener Cards:** Used to statistically test perception beyond chance.

While early studies claimed significant results (Rhine, 1934), methodological critiques and failed replications have left ESP as a controversial and unresolved field.

3.8 Psychokinesis and Mind-Matter Interaction

Psychokinesis (PK) refers to the ability to influence physical objects using mental intent.

Micro vs. Macro PK:

- **Micro-PK:** Subtle influence on systems (e.g., random number generators).
- **Macro-PK:** Observable effects like bending spoons or moving objects.

Research Findings:

- Studies at institutions such as the PEAR Lab (Princeton Engineering Anomalies Research) reported small statistical deviations, though critics argued these lacked practical significance or reproducibility (Jahn et al., 2000).

Field Reports:

Accounts of moving furniture, levitating objects, or physical manifestations are often anecdotal and lack controlled documentation.

3.9 Cryptids and Biological Anomalies

Cryptozoology, while often dismissed by mainstream science, intersects with paranormal investigation when dealing with alleged sightings of creatures not recognized by biology.

Notable Cryptids:

- Bigfoot / Sasquatch (North America)
- Yeti (Himalayas)
- Loch Ness Monster (Scotland)
- Mokele-Mbembe (Central Africa)

Methodological Issues:

Many cryptid reports suffer from lack of physical evidence, hoaxes, and unreliable witness testimony. However, the persistence of such legends across time and geography continues to fuel speculative biological inquiry.

3.10 UFOs and Anomalous Aerial Phenomena

Unidentified Aerial Phenomena (UAPs), formerly referred to as UFOs, represent a longstanding category of unexplained visual and radar-tracked anomalies.

Key Features:

- High velocity, non-inertial motion.
- Sudden acceleration and directional shifts.
- Apparent awareness of observer behavior.

Institutional Attention:

In recent years, government agencies such as the U.S. Department of Defense have acknowledged UAPs through reports such as the 2021 Preliminary Assessment by the Office of the Director of National Intelligence (ODNI). While not considered inherently paranormal, their unexplained nature aligns them with the broader scope of anomalistic investigation.

A coherent classification system allows paranormal investigators to systematically observe, compare, and interpret phenomena. While scientific skepticism and methodological rigor remain essential, an understanding of these diverse categories helps clarify investigative focus, adapt tools and techniques, and avoid interpretive error.

In subsequent chapters, we will examine how this typology informs the practical conduct of field investigations, from preparation to analysis.

Chapter Four

Tools and Technology in Investigation

4.1 Introduction: The Role of Instrumentation

The use of technology in paranormal investigations is indispensable. While anecdotal evidence dominates many reports, empirical tools provide the potential for objective data collection, pattern recognition, and the testing of hypotheses. Proper use of instrumentation enhances the credibility of investigations and facilitates reproducibility, which are central tenets of any scientific approach.

Though paranormal research remains on the margins of mainstream science, its methodological evolution has increasingly emphasized measurable data. The tools listed in this chapter are employed not to prove the existence of paranormal phenomena per se, but to monitor anomalies that might correlate with reported events.

4.2 Electronic Voice Phenomena (EVP) Recorders and Audio Analysis

Definition:

EVP refers to anomalous voice-like sounds, typically inaudible during recording but discernible upon playback. These are considered potential spirit communications or residual energy signatures.

Equipment:

- **Digital audio recorders:** Preferably with high sampling rates ($\geq$96 kHz).
- **External condenser microphones:** Reduce internal noise and improve frequency sensitivity.
- **Audio analysis software:** Programs such as Audacity, Adobe Audition, or specialized spectral analysis tools (e.g., Sonic Visualiser).

Protocol:

1. Conduct baseline environmental recording in silence.

2. Use clear vocal questions with spacing for response.

3. Note ambient conditions and external noise sources.

4. Analyze recordings using waveform and spectral tools to detect anomalies.

Critical Consideration:

Pareidolia (the tendency to perceive patterns in random noise) and contamination from radio frequency interference must be carefully controlled.

4.3 Electromagnetic Field (EMF) Detectors

Purpose:

EMF detectors measure fluctuations in electromagnetic fields, which some theorists believe may accompany or indicate the presence of paranormal entities.

Types:

- Single-axis detectors: Detect EMF in one direction.
- Tri-axis detectors: Provide more accurate field representation.
- Multi-function meters: Combine EMF, temperature, and humidity sensors.

Common Models:

- K-II EMF Meter.
- Trifield Natural EM Meter.
- MEL Meter (with EMF + thermocouple).

Usage:

1. Establish a baseline in all rooms.
2. Investigate spikes or anomalies, documenting timing and location.
3. Correlate EMF changes with witness experiences or other instrumentation.

Limitations:

EMF readings can be affected by nearby electronics, power lines, and wireless devices. Cross-validation with environmental surveys is essential.

4.4 Infrared Cameras and Night Vision Technology

Purpose:

Many reported paranormal events occur in low-light conditions. Infrared (IR) cameras allow visual recording in complete darkness using

IR illumination.

Equipment:

- **Full-spectrum cameras:** Capable of recording across visible, UV, and IR wavelengths.
- **Static IR surveillance systems:** Allow for continuous multi-angle coverage.
- **Thermal imaging cameras:** Detect heat signatures and temperature variations.

Advantages:

- Detect unseen motion or temperature fluctuations.
- Enable post-investigation review of visual anomalies.
- Allow for non-intrusive surveillance over long periods.

Cautions:

Visual anomalies may result from IR reflection, dust, or lens aberrations. Investigators must cross-reference footage with logs and sensor data.

4.5 Spirit Boxes and Frequency Sweep Devices

Description:

Spirit boxes rapidly scan AM or FM radio frequencies, producing white noise over which fragmented words may be interpreted. Some investigators believe spirits can manipulate this energy to communicate.

Models:

- P-SB7 and P-SB11 Spirit Boxes.
- Custom-built frequency sweepers with adjustable sweep rates.

Methods:

1. Conduct baseline sweep to rule out known broadcasts.
2. Ask direct questions and record responses.
3. Evaluate consistency, contextual relevance, and timing.

Scientific Challenges:

Skeptics argue that random words from radio broadcasts or audio pareidolia account for perceived messages. Controlled conditions are essential to reduce bias.

4.6 Motion Detectors and Trigger Objects

Purpose:

Motion detectors and trigger objects are passive monitoring tools used to detect physical movement in areas where activity is suspected.

Tools:

- PIR (passive infrared) motion sensors.
- Pressure-sensitive mats.
- Laser grids with motion interruption alarms.

Trigger Object Protocol:

1. Select object relevant to reported entity (e.g., toy for child spirit).

2. Document placement using photography and coordinate grids.

3. Use time-lapse or motion-triggered cameras to monitor disturbance.

Advantages:

Simple, low-cost tools that can yield strong visual or movement evidence when properly documented.

4.7 Environmental Sensors: Temperature, Barometric Pressure, and Humidity

Unexplained "cold spots" are frequently reported in hauntings. While perception can be misleading, objective measurement allows verification of environmental anomalies.

Recommended Devices:

- Digital thermometers (with infrared and ambient sensors).
- Data loggers: Continuously record environmental changes.
- Barometric pressure meters: Detect shifts potentially related to sealed environments or structural anomalies.

Usage:

- Establish controlled environmental maps.
- Note sudden drops or increases during investigative sessions.
- Cross-check with anecdotal reports.

Critical Thinking:

Many reported cold spots can be traced to airflow, insulation gaps, or psychological suggestion. Data collection should aim to explain, not confirm, phenomena.

4.8 Dowsing Rods and Pendulums (Historical Tools)

Background:

Dowsing rods and pendulums have been used historically for spirit communication and energy detection. These tools rely on subtle hand movements and ideomotor responses.

Method:

- **Dowsing rods:** Typically held parallel and respond to unseen "energies" by crossing or spreading apart.
- **Pendulums:** Suspended objects used to answer yes/no questions through directional swings.

Scientific Evaluation:

Numerous studies attribute dowsing results to unconscious motor behavior rather than external forces. While controversial, these tools remain popular among some traditional investigators.

4.9 Software and Digital Evidence Management

Data Integrity:

Digital tools support structured documentation, improve accuracy, and facilitate peer review.

Software Types:

- **Audio Analysis:** Audacity, GoldWave, Raven Pro.
- **Video Review:** VLC, DaVinci Resolve, time-coded annotation platforms.
- **Data Logging:** Excel, SPSS, or custom-built databases for environmental and observational data.
- **Mapping and Visualization:** GIS software for mapping phenomena location and frequency.

Best Practices:

- Timestamp all data points.
- Use consistent naming conventions.
- Secure backup of raw and processed files.
- Maintain detailed metadata and version histories.

4.10 Custom and Emerging Technology

Innovations:

- **Mobile apps:** EMF detectors, EVP analyzers, augmented-reality spirit viewers (not scientifically validated).
- **IoT-integrated devices:** Automated sensor networks for environmental tracking.
- **Artificial Intelligence (AI):** Early-stage use in anomaly detection in video/audio files.

Ethical and Methodological Concerns:

- Apps often lack empirical validity and can generate false positives.
- Investigators should avoid over-reliance on consumer tools without validation.

4.11 Equipment Calibration and Testing

For results to be reliable, all tools must undergo regular calibration. This includes:

- Testing against known values.
- Documenting instrument sensitivity and limitations.
- Field validation to eliminate error sources.

Calibration ensures measurement integrity and aids in filtering out background noise, environmental interference, or technical artifacts.

Tools and technology are integral to contemporary paranormal investigations. They offer the potential for rigorous data collection and pattern recognition—provided they are used systematically, ethically, and with a critical awareness of their limitations.

However, no device alone can validate the existence of paranormal phenomena. They are best understood as aids to observation, forming part of a broader methodological framework that incorporates environmental awareness, critical thinking, and interdisciplinary analysis.

Chapter Five

Methodology of a Paranormal Investigation

5.1 Introduction

The field of paranormal investigation lacks a unified protocol or universally recognized methodology. However, based on best practices adopted by researchers, psychical societies, and experienced investigators, it is possible to outline a replicable and academically responsible framework for inquiry. This chapter details that process, beginning with pre-investigation preparation and concluding with post-investigation analysis and reporting.

5.2 Case Intake and Preliminary Research

A. Client Interviews

In residential or institutional cases, the first step involves conducting structured interviews with witnesses or clients.

Goals:

- Establish a timeline of events.
- Understand witness interpretations and emotional states.
- Identify possible environmental or psychological explanations.

Best Practices:

- Use open-ended questions.
- Avoid suggestive or leading language.
- Record (with consent) for transcription and content analysis.

B. Historical and Environmental Research

Every location has a contextual history—architectural, cultural, and geographical—that may influence reported activity.

Sources:

- Local archives and property records.
- Newspaper databases and police reports.

- Ethnographic data (folklore, religious practices, community narratives).

This contextual backdrop assists in evaluating whether phenomena may be tied to environmental, cultural, or social variables.

5.3 Forming an Investigation Team

A. Ideal Team Roles

1. **Lead Investigator:** Coordinates methodology, ensures consistency.
2. **Technical Specialist:** Manages equipment and data integrity.
3. **Research Analyst:** Handles historical data and comparative analysis.
4. **Field Documentarian:** Records audio/video, maintains logbooks.
5. **Client Liaison:** Manages communication and support.

B. Team Composition Considerations

- Avoid teams larger than necessary; excessive personnel may Contaminate data.
- Emphasize diversity of skills—scientific literacy, empathy, and skepticism.
- Ensure all members understand ethical protocols and confidentiality agreements.

5.4 Pre-Investigation Baseline Assessment

Prior to any nighttime or formal investigation, a baseline environmental assessment must be conducted.

A. Environmental Survey

Measurements:

- Ambient temperature.
- EMF levels (low and high frequency).
- Barometric pressure and humidity.
- Airflow (ventilation patterns).

Methods:

- Use grid-based mapping to document fluctuations.
- Repeat measurements at different times of day.

B. Psychological and Physiological Context

If the location is inhabited, document:

- Sleep patterns, mental health diagnoses (with consent).
- Medications or substances that may cause hallucinations.
- History of trauma or grief (common in haunting reports).

5.5 Design of the Investigation Protocol

A structured plan is critical to avoid bias, ensure reproducibility, and enhance scientific rigor.

A. Research Questions

Define clear, testable questions:

- "Are there anomalous EMF changes during specific time windows?"
- "Is there audio evidence unexplainable by natural or technological means?"

B. Hypotheses

Establish null hypotheses (e.g., "There will be no significant EMF change beyond environmental norms").

C. Variable Control

- Eliminate or document all sources of contamination (e.g., power outlets, mobile phones, pets).
- Establish time stamps for all investigative sessions.
- Mark positions of team members and cameras.

5.6 Conducting the Investigation

A. Initial Walkthrough (Lights On)

- Confirm structural safety.
- Tag potential sources of interference (mirrors, electronics).
- Test equipment functionality.

B. Main Session (Lights Off)

Procedure:

- Operate under minimal noise and light.
- Use fixed-position cameras and microphones.
- Space out EVP sessions to prevent biasing results.

Sample EVP Protocol:

1. Introduce time, location, and all present individuals.
2. Ask neutral, clear questions.
3. Leave 15–30 seconds of silence between each.
4. Document time stamps, background noise, and personal sensations.

C. Trigger Object Tests

Place objects (balls, coins, toys) in camera-monitored positions and document any movement.

5.7 Observational Documentation

A. Field Log

Maintain a standardized logbook:

- Room diagrams.
- EMF/temperature readings.
- Team locations and activities.
- Audio/video file IDs.

B. Subjective Experience Log

While subjective reports are not empirical evidence, they can guide further analysis:

- Log who experienced what, when, and under what conditions.
- Cross-reference with environmental data (e.g., "EMF spike at 11:42 PM when Investigator A felt cold pressure on arm").

5.8 Data Integrity and Contamination Control

A. Tagging and Annotation

Use vocal or digital tagging for each session (e.g., "Start EVP – Kitchen – 10:22 PM – Investigator 1, 2").

B. Secure Data Storage

- Backup all recordings in multiple formats.
- Use write-once media (DVD-R) or checksum-protected drives.
- Retain raw footage along with annotated versions.

C. Contamination Sources

- Electronic interference (phones, walkie-talkies).
- Air vents and drafts.
- Wildlife or insects.
- Psychological suggestion (e.g., priming from horror imagery).

5.9 Post-Investigation Analysis

A. Review and Correlation

Review all collected data methodically:

- Compare environmental readings to witness reports.
- Analyze audio/video files for anomalies.
- Use software tools to isolate frequencies and eliminate false positives.

B. Criteria for Evidence Classification:

1. Class A: Clearly audible/visible and contextually relevant.
2. Class B: Anomalous but ambiguous or distorted.
3. Class C: Inconclusive due to interference or subjectivity.

C. Peer Review:

Invite third-party investigators or specialists (e.g., sound engineers, physicists) to review findings without knowing client history—a form of blind analysis.

5.10 Reporting and Presentation of Findings

A. Investigative Report Structure

1. Executive Summary
2. Background and Objectives
3. Methodology

4. Data Collected
5. Analysis
6. Findings and Interpretation
7. Conclusion and Recommendations
8. Appendices (logs, maps, transcripts)

B. Visual and Audio Supplements

- Include annotated photographs, spectrograms, and logbook scans.
- Time-code key audio events and correlate with environmental data.

C. Communication with Clients

- Present findings respectfully and neutrally.
- Avoid declarative statements ("This proves ghosts exist").
- Emphasize that no conclusion is definitive without replication and further study.

5.11 Summary

Paranormal investigation demands more than intuition or gadgetry—it requires methodological discipline, ethical clarity, and systematic observation. While definitive proof of paranormal phenomena remains elusive, credible investigation methods allow for legitimate exploration, improved understanding, and responsible representation of anomalous claims.

In the chapters that follow, we will build upon this foundation with real-world case studies that demonstrate how methodology, theory, and field practice intersect.

Pre-Investigation: It is important because it includes research, getting permission, getting documents ready etc. for private property we can conduct video or telephonic conversation with the client to know the every single details regarding the haunting, know the place history, incidents that took place and note down and draft series of questions for main investigation, check all the devices working properly or not, once we finish with client we need to do our own secondary research like surfing on net, searching local library and meeting local people to capture their views. Take permission to investigate and get the documents signed from client and release of photos and videos on social media platforms. Once information is gathered visit the property at day time which gives us the inside out view of property take preliminary pictures of key places and objects and also mark them so during main investigation we get an edge. We also do small spiritual ritual like imagine by closing the eyes a white beam which can create for your protection and feel strongly that during investigation it is your protection shield from bad & evil. Here spirit also become familiar with our presence. Always seek permission from current property owner in writing before conducting paranormal investigation. **Main Investigation:** Here we start our investigation by introducing ourselves to the spirit by saying our name, introduce your teammates, etc. next steps depends on investigators and the situations but always be professional and talk like professional and don't be afraid. Start EMF sensors first and ask some general questions and ask the claims you have gathered if they are ready for EVP sessions, start EVP recorders and record the session. If you have claims of apparitions or shadows or movements, use motion sensor and so on. Always be calm and be clear what you are asking & have patience. **Post Investigation:** Make sure to say goodbye to the spirit world, if we are not performing the cleansing. Repeat the following sentence. **"Thank you for the replies. You are not allowed to follow me back home. This is where you belong and this is where you stay. Do not follow me or anyone. Goodbye."**

Always ask questions during investigation:

a.) What is your name?
b.) What year it is?
c.) How many of you are here?
d.) Are you angry?
e.) Are you happy?
f.) Are you male or female?
g.) Are you afraid?
h.) Why are you here?
i.) How did you passed away?

j.) Are you aware of your death?
k.) Any massage that you would like to give?

Additional Tips:

1. Maintain Objectivity: Approach investigations with a neutral mindset.

2. Respect the Location: Treat the location and clients with respect.

3. Continuing Education: Stay updated on new equipment, techniques, and research.

4. Teamwork: Collaborate with team members to ensure a successful investigation.

5. Cleansing: Before closing the investigation you must perform the cleansing activity at the property.

Remember, paranormal investigations require patience, dedication, and a systematic approach. By following these protocols and procedures, you'll be well-equipped to conduct a thorough and effective investigation.

Chapter Six

Ethics and Responsibilities in Paranormal Investigation

6.1 Introduction

Paranormal investigation, while often considered a fringe or pseudoscientific pursuit, operates at the intersection of human psychology, spirituality, belief, and science. This delicate position places unique ethical obligations upon investigators. Regardless of one's personal beliefs, the treatment of clients, handling of sensitive data, and representation of findings must adhere to clear moral and professional standards.

This chapter outlines the ethical dimensions that underpin credible, respectful, and socially responsible investigative work.

6.2 Foundational Ethical Principles

Three core principles underpin the ethics of paranormal research:

A. Respect for Persons

- Upholding the dignity, privacy, and emotional well-being of all individuals involved.
- Ensuring informed consent for interviews, recordings, and investigation procedures.
- Maintaining confidentiality and respecting spiritual or religious beliefs.

B. Beneficence and Non-Maleficence

- Minimizing harm—psychological, social, or physical—through careful conduct.
- Avoiding sensationalism or fear mongering, especially in emotionally vulnerable environments.

C. Integrity and Honesty

- Ensuring accuracy in data collection and interpretation.

- Avoiding exaggeration, deception, or fabrication of evidence.
- Clearly differentiating between theory, speculation, and evidence-based claims.

6.3 Informed Consent

A. Client Consent

Before initiating any investigation, written consent must be obtained from:

- Property owners or tenants.
- Individuals featured in recordings or interviews.
- Guardians of minors (where applicable).

Consent should cover:

- Purpose and scope of investigation.
- Data collection methods and equipment used.
- Use and storage of audio, video, and written data.
- Terms of publication or sharing of findings.

B. Ongoing Consent

Consent is not a one-time event—it must be re-evaluated if conditions change, particularly if:

- New evidence arises with potential psychological impact.
- Findings are to be published or publicized.
- The client withdraws consent.

6.4 Confidentiality and Data Protection

A. Data Anonymization

Unless explicitly permitted, all identifying information—names, locations, personal histories—should be anonymized in:

- Written reports.
- Public lectures or media appearances.
- Online postings and videos.

B. Data Storage

- Raw and processed data must be stored securely, with backups and encryption where appropriate.

- Establish clear data retention policies—how long material is stored and under what conditions it is destroyed.

C. Third-Party Disclosure

Data should never be shared with third parties (media outlets, entertainment producers, rival investigators) without explicit consent and purpose clarification.

6.5 Psychological and Emotional Sensitivity

Paranormal experiences often emerge during times of personal crisis—bereavement, trauma, or spiritual searching.

Responsibilities of Investigators:

- Refrain from making grand metaphysical claims or interpretations (e.g., declaring a spirit's identity).
- Avoid reinforcing delusions or irrational fears.
- Offer referrals to mental health professionals when appropriate.
- Validate the experience without necessarily validating its cause.

Red Flags:

- Clients exhibiting paranoia, hallucinations, or delusional thinking.
- Individuals with severe anxiety, depression, or grief-driven behaviors.

In such cases, a collaborative approach with counselors or therapists may be more ethical than continuing the investigation.

6.6 Skepticism, Bias, and Intellectual Honesty

Paranormal investigators must constantly be aware of:

- **Confirmation bias:** Favoring evidence that supports one's beliefs.
- **Apophenia:** Perceiving connections or patterns where none exist.
- **Over-interpretation:** Assigning paranormal explanations prematurely.

Best Practices:

- Document all results—anomalous or not.

- Avoid manipulating evidence to support personal theories.
- Distinguish between subjective experiences and objective data.
- Embrace peer review, especially from skeptical or interdisciplinary audiences.

6.7 Avoiding Exploitation and Commercialization

The rise of television shows, social media influencers, and paranormal tourism has led to widespread commodification of the unexplained.

Unethical Practices to Avoid:

- Charging clients excessive fees for investigations or "cleansings."
- Selling talismans, rituals, or proprietary devices under paranormal pretexts.
- Creating dramatic, false narratives to gain public attention or media deals.

Ethical investigators should:

- Operate on a voluntary, nonprofit, or transparent fee basis.
- Decline involvement in cases where integrity may be compromised.
- Focus on truth-seeking, not entertainment.

6.8 Cultural and Religious Sensitivity

Paranormal experiences are often interpreted through cultural and religious lenses. An academically responsible approach respects these frameworks without appropriating or diminishing them.

Guidelines:

- Understand the local cosmology (e.g., djinn in Islamic cultures, ancestral spirits in African or Indigenous traditions).
- Collaborate with cultural custodians, elders, or religious leaders where appropriate.
- Avoid dismissing beliefs as "superstition" or attempting to impose Western scientific models unilaterally.

Example:

An investigator entering a household in rural India reporting a preta (wandering spirit) must understand the Hindu death rites and cultural narratives surrounding spirit possession before proposing EVP sessions or EMF scans.

6.9 Professional Conduct in Public and Media Spaces

Investigators often interact with the public through:

- Social media platforms.
- Paranormal conferences.
- Online video or podcast content.

Code of Conduct:

- Refrain from publishing unverified evidence.
- Avoid mockery, ridicule, or performative skepticism.
- Use disclaimers to distinguish theory, belief, and evidence.
- Respect other researchers and avoid competitive hostility or "debunking wars."

Professionalism strengthens both public trust and interdisciplinary collaboration.

6.10 Ethical Dilemmas and Decision-Making

Paranormal investigation often involves ambiguous situations where ethical answers are not clear-cut.

Case Studies of Ethical Dilemmas:

1. Client insists on exorcism by the team – If team members are not qualified,
decline and refer to appropriate spiritual authorities.
2. Evidence suggests potential fraud by the client – Document neutrally, avoid
confrontation, and end the case respectfully.
3. Historic site requests a promotional investigation but asks for sensational content – Prioritize truth over narrative enhancement.

When in doubt, investigators should consult peers, ethicists, or professional boards where applicable.

6.11 Establishing a Code of Ethics

Organizations and independent teams should establish written ethical guidelines. Components may include:

- Confidentiality agreements.
- Media policies.
- Client interaction protocols.
- Evidence handling procedures.
- Team member accountability measures.

Publicizing this code demonstrates professionalism and helps build public and scholarly credibility.

6.12 Summary

Ethics are not an optional consideration in paranormal investigation—they are its backbone. Without integrity, no amount of data or equipment can lend credibility to a field already under skepticism. By prioritizing human dignity, intellectual honesty, and cultural sensitivity, investigators can not only protect those they serve but elevate the standard of their craft.

Chapter Seven

Case Studies in Paranormal Investigation

7.1 Introduction

Case studies offer valuable insight into the applied methodology and ethical dimensions of paranormal investigation. Whether drawn from historical records, contemporary investigations, or composite patterns, each case provides opportunities to examine the interplay between subjective experience, environmental data, and investigative technique. This chapter presents six selected case studies—three historically documented and three composite scenarios—designed to illustrate best practices, analytical challenges, and methodological variation in the field.

7.2 Historical Case Studies

Case Study A: The Enfield Poltergeist (1977–1979, London, UK)

Background:

The Enfield case remains one of the most widely publicized and debated poltergeist investigations of the 20th century. Centered on a council house in North London, the case involved two sisters, aged 11 and 13, who reported unexplained knocking sounds, levitations, and possession-like behavior.

Investigative Bodies:

- Society for Psychical Research (SPR)
- Maurice Grosse and Guy Lyon Playfair

Methods Used:

- Continuous audio recording
- Still photography and infrared surveillance
- Interviews and physical measurements

Findings:

- Dozens of witnesses reported objects moving or flying across rooms.

- Tape recordings captured knocking patterns and guttural voice phenomena.
- Critics pointed out possible child fabrication and staged scenes.

Analysis:

While the case includes moments suggestive of fraud, it also produced anomalous data that defied conventional explanation. Methodologically, the investigation was notable for its duration (over a year) and mixed instrumentation. However, ethical concerns arose regarding the pressure placed on child witnesses and media involvement.

Case Study B: The Amherst Mystery (1878–1879, Nova Scotia, Canada)

Background:

Ester Cox, a teenage girl living with her family, reportedly experienced violent poltergeist activity following a traumatic emotional incident.

Phenomena:

- Fires starting spontaneously
- Writing appearing on walls
- Furniture movement
- Vocalized threats from unseen entities

Investigation:

- Local clergymen and journalists
- Short-term physical surveillance
- Spiritual medium involvement

Findings:

No hard evidence was collected under controlled conditions, but numerous community members validated Ester's claims. Her physical condition often deteriorated during activity.

Analysis:

This case illustrates the difficulty of 19th-century investigations where empirical methods were absent. It also highlights how trauma and belief intersect in paranormal claims.

Case Study C: The Borley Rectory Haunting (1929–1939, Essex, UK)

Background:

Described as "the most haunted house in England," Borley Rectory gained notoriety due to ghost sightings, phantom footsteps, wall writings, and mysterious sounds.

Lead Investigator:

Harry Price (noted paranormal researcher)

Methods:

- Extensive journaling
- Séances and Ouija boards
- Presence of observers and rotating guest witnesses

Findings:

- Wall writing appeared requesting help from a "nun."
- Objects moved in the absence of people.
- Critics accused Price of orchestrating or exaggerating events.

Analysis:

The case reflects the early evolution of paranormal methodology—rich in documentation but lacking environmental controls. It also raised questions about investigator influence on phenomena and the potential for confirmation bias.

7.3 Fictionalized Composite Case Studies

The following composite cases are fictional but constructed using consistent patterns reported across dozens of documented investigations worldwide. They reflect commonly encountered phenomena, ethical decisions, and investigative limitations.

Case Study D: The Whispering Library (India, 2015)

Setting:

A 100-year-old government library in West Bengal reportedly haunted by the ghost of its first librarian. Staff claimed hearing whispered warnings after dusk, with rare books found rearranged or torn.

Client Concern:

Loss of historical artifacts and staff refusal to work night shifts.

Investigation Plan:

- 3-night baseline EMF and sound recording sweep
- Historical research on the building's construction and original staff
- Controlled EVP (Electronic Voice Phenomena) sessions

Findings:

- Audible whispering recorded twice—both matching no external source.
- Historical logs revealed the original librarian died during a cholera outbreak and was buried on-site.
- EMF readings spiked near the records section, possibly due to hidden wiring.

Resolution:

Recommending environmental cleaning and introducing night guards. Activity decreased after the structure's rewiring.

Ethical Analysis:

The team avoided claims of spirit identity and focused on observable data. They communicated respectfully with staff and refrained from public disclosure due to governmental confidentiality agreements.

Case Study E: The Desert House Apparition (Namibia, 2018)

Setting:

An isolated bungalow near the Namib Desert inhabited by a family of four. A translucent female figure was reportedly seen moving across windows at dawn.

Investigation Methods:

- Motion-sensitive thermal cameras
- Psychological profiling of witnesses
- Lunar cycle correlation analysis

Findings:

- A thermal camera captured a humanoid figure on two consecutive mornings at 5:15 AM.

- The figure dissipated within 3 seconds and emitted no heat signature.
- Further analysis revealed temperature inversions from desert winds could create optical illusions.

Conclusion:

While the thermal recordings could not be fully explained, environmental distortion remained a probable cause. The apparition did not reappear in the months that followed.

Lessons Learned:

This case highlighted the importance of integrating atmospheric science into fieldwork. Investigators maintained neutrality and shared findings with local scientific institutions.

Case Study F: The Possession of Mrs. G (USA, 2020)

Background:

A 43-year-old schoolteacher in Pennsylvania reported loss of memory, involuntary speech in unfamiliar languages, and violent outbursts. A local church suspected demonic possession and refused further involvement.

Investigation Protocol:

- Interviews with family and clergy
- EEG scans and psychological referral
- Joint inquiry with clinical psychologists and religious scholars

Findings:

- Neurological tests showed no abnormalities.
- Linguistic analysis suggested the foreign language was phonetically similar to Aramaic.
- The subject entered dissociative states but could later recall details of the episodes.

Outcome:

The case was classified as a dissociative identity disorder with culturally-influenced manifestations. No spiritual interventions were attempted by the investigators.

Ethical Evaluation:

The team prioritized the subject's mental health, refused exorcism requests, and coordinated with licensed professionals. This model respects both the cultural and clinical dimensions of such cases.

7.4 Summary

These case studies serve multiple pedagogical functions:

- Demonstrating how theory and field methods interrelate.
- Highlighting the ethical spectrum from privacy to clinical care.
- Encouraging critical thinking when faced with anomalous evidence.

In sum, while not all cases yield clear answers, they contribute to a growing body of investigative literature that prizes rigor, skepticism, and respect. The next chapter will explore the tools and technologies used in such investigations—from traditional methods to emerging digital techniques.

Chapter Eight

Specialized Areas in Paranormal Research

8.1 Introduction

While traditional paranormal investigations often focus on hauntings and unexplained phenomena in domestic or institutional settings, the broader field of paranormal research encompasses diverse sub-disciplines that extend far beyond ghosts and spirits. These specialized domains reflect efforts to study a wide spectrum of anomalous phenomena, including psychical abilities, cryptids, demonic influence, unidentified aerial phenomena (UAPs), and near-death experiences (NDEs).

In this chapter, we provide an academically grounded overview of these specialized fields, offering foundational concepts, terminologies, historical context, and current investigative approaches. Each domain operates at the fringes of mainstream science, but many are supported by structured methodologies and growing databases of case evidence.

8.2 Parapsychology

Definition:

Parapsychology is the scientific study of purported psychic phenomena, including Extra Sensory Perception (ESP), Psychokinesis (PK), and telepathy. Researchers in this field aim to apply rigorous experimental and statistical methods to investigate human consciousness and its interaction with the physical world.

Key Concepts:

- **ESP (Extrasensory Perception):** Reception of information without use of the known senses. Includes telepathy, clairvoyance, and precognition.
- **PK (Psychokinesis):** The ability to affect physical objects using mental intention alone.

Methods:

- Random number generators (for micro-PK experiments)
- Ganzfeld procedures (telepathy experiments)
- Zener cards (ESP testing)
- Controlled lab environments to eliminate sensory leakage

Academic Perspective:

Although parapsychology is not widely accepted in mainstream psychology, notable institutions such as the Rhine Research Center and PEAR (Princeton Engineering Anomalies Research) have conducted decades-long experiments. Meta-analyses continue to provoke debate on whether results indicate real effects or statistical anomalies.

8.3 Cryptozoology

Definition:

Cryptozoology is the study of animals whose existence is not recognized by mainstream biology. These entities—termed "cryptids"—include Bigfoot, the Loch Ness Monster, Chupacabra, and other culturally significant creatures.

Historical Roots:

The discipline gained momentum in the mid-20th century with figures like Bernard Heuvelmans and Ivan T. Sanderson. Some cryptids, like the okapi and the coelacanth, were once considered mythical but were later confirmed to exist.

Methods:

- Eyewitness interviews and folklore analysis
- Physical footprint and scat analysis
- Remote trail cameras and drone surveillance
- Geographic Information Systems (GIS) for mapping sightings

Scientific Challenges:

- Lack of biological specimens or verifiable remains
- Reliance on anecdotal data
- Difficulty in distinguishing folklore from factual reports

Relation to Paranormal Investigation:

While often viewed as separate from ghost research, cryptozoology shares methodological overlaps with field investigations—particularly in rural or wilderness settings where alleged sightings occur.

8.4 Demonology

Definition:

Demonology is the study of demons or malevolent spiritual entities and their manifestations. While often associated with religious doctrine, contemporary demonology involves interdisciplinary study encompassing theology, folklore, psychology, and paranormal investigation.

Key Characteristics of Alleged Demonic Activity:

- Oppressive atmospheres
- Unexplained aggression or personality shifts
- Speaking in unknown languages (glossolalia or xenoglossy)
- Physical marks (scratches, burns) without apparent cause
- Religious resistance (entities react to sacred symbols)

Investigation Protocols:

- Collaboration with religious authorities (e.g., exorcists)
- Psychological assessment of afflicted individuals
- Recording environmental anomalies (temperature drops, EMF spikes)
- Ethical considerations: risk of mental health misdiagnosis

Academic Challenges:

Demonology is difficult to approach empirically due to its theological grounding. Nonetheless, serious investigators must be familiar with spiritual frameworks across cultures to interpret cases responsibly.

8.5 Near-Death Experiences (NDEs)

Definition:

An NDE is a profound psychological experience reported by individuals who were close to death or clinically dead before being resuscitated. Common themes include feelings of peace, out-of-body experiences, tunnel vision, encounters with spiritual beings, and life reviews.

Common Characteristics (as identified by Dr. Raymond Moody):

- A sense of detachment from the body.

- Movement through a dark tunnel toward a light.
- Intense emotional warmth and peace.
- Encounters with deceased relatives or religious figures.
- Reluctance to return to physical life.

Methods of Study:

- Qualitative interviews with experiencers
- Cross-cultural analysis
- Neurobiological correlations (oxygen deprivation, temporal lobe activity)
- Longitudinal studies on post-NDE psychological changes

Scientific and Philosophical Implications:

NDEs raise questions about consciousness, death, and the afterlife. Though often dismissed as neurochemical responses, the consistency of reports across cultures and belief systems has drawn the attention of consciousness researchers and physicians.

8.6 Ufology and UAP Research

Definition:

Ufology is the study of unidentified flying objects (UFOs), now more commonly referred to as unidentified aerial phenomena (UAPs). This field investigates sightings, encounters, and abduction claims, and increasingly overlaps with government and military interests.

Recent Developments:

- U.S. Department of Defense's establishment of the All-domain Anomaly Resolution Office (AARO).
- Declassification of military encounters (e.g., USS Nimitz incident).
- Congressional hearings on UAP transparency.

Types of Encounters (Hynek Classification):

- Nocturnal Lights
- Daylight Discs
- Radar/Visual Sightings
- Close Encounters of the First–Fourth Kind (visual to abduction)

Investigation Techniques:

- Video and radar analysis
- Witness credibility evaluations
- Meteorological cross-referencing
- Satellite imagery and sensor analysis

Academic and Defense Contexts:

While still marginalized, UAP research is beginning to gain institutional credibility due to national security implications and consistent anomalous data from credible sources (e.g., pilots, radar technicians).

8.7 Consciousness Studies and Anomalous Cognition

Definition:

This emerging field explores the potential of human consciousness to access or interact with information beyond conventional sensory mechanisms. Topics include remote viewing, precognitive dreams, and non-local awareness.

Notable Research Projects:

- **Stargate Project:** U.S. military-funded remote viewing initiative
- **Global Consciousness Project:** Random Event Generators responding to global events (e.g., 9/11, tsunamis)

Research Tools:

- Statistical randomness analysis
- Double-blind remote viewing trials
- Controlled dream journals with predictive scoring
- FMRI and EEG for altered state mapping

Implications for Paranormal Investigators:

Understanding consciousness-related phenomena may offer insights into psychic experiences reported during investigations (e.g., medium ship, intuitive perceptions). It also challenges materialist models of perception and cognition.

8.8 Conclusion

Each specialized area within paranormal research offers its own methodologies, theoretical frameworks, and epistemological challenges.

While mainstream science often views these domains with skepticism, investigators must be aware of these fields in order to approach cases with cultural sensitivity, interdisciplinary awareness, and ethical responsibility.

As the field matures, collaboration with psychologists, neuroscientists, anthropologists, and theologians may improve the validity and depth of paranormal research. Investigators who pursue a cross-disciplinary approach will be better equipped to interpret complex phenomena with rigor and respect.

Chapter Nine

Building Your Investigator's Toolkit

9.1 Introduction

A systematic approach to paranormal investigation requires more than curiosity—it demands precision, preparation, and appropriate instrumentation. The "toolkit" of a paranormal investigator includes not only electronic devices and data collection instruments but also methodological frameworks, documentation tools, and ethical guidelines.

In this chapter, we examine the essential tools—both physical and conceptual—used in contemporary investigations. We explore the science behind each tool, its intended application, its limitations, and the procedures for calibration and use. Whether in a haunted residence or a historical battlefield, the investigator's toolkit should be adapted to context, research objectives, and environmental conditions.

9.2 Categorizing Tools: Physical vs. Conceptual

Investigative tools can be classified into two broad categories:

- Physical Tools (Instrumental Devices)

These are tangible items used for measurement, documentation, or detection of phenomena.

- Conceptual Tools (Cognitive/Methodological)

These include frameworks for observation, documentation protocols, cultural sensitivity guides, and psychological evaluation checklists.

A balanced investigation requires integrating both categories for scientific rigor and human sensitivity.

9.3 Essential Physical Tools

1. **Electromagnetic Field (EMF) Detectors**

- **Function:** Measures fluctuations in electromagnetic fields, which some researchers correlate with spirit activity.
- **Types:** Single-axis, tri-field, and data-logging meters
- **Scientific Use:** Identifies faulty wiring or hidden appliances that

could cause false perceptions

- **Limitations:** Sensitive to mobile phones, routers, and metal

2. **Digital Audio Recorders**

- **Function:** Capture Electronic Voice Phenomena (EVPs)
- **Specs:** High bit-rate, low noise floor, omni-directional microphones
- **Best Practices:** Record baseline silence; avoid overlapping speech; timestamp entries

3. **Infrared (IR) and Full-Spectrum Cameras**

- **Use:** Capture anomalies invisible to the naked eye in dark or low-light environments
- **Enhancements:** Motion-activated recording; night-vision mode
- **Artifacts:** Lens flares, dust particles, and camera noise often misinterpreted

4. **Thermographic (Thermal Imaging) Cameras**

- **Function:** Detect heat signatures to reveal anomalies (cold or hot spots)
- **Use Case:** Identifying sudden temperature drops correlated with entity manifestation
- **Caution:** Air conditioning, drafts, and reflective surfaces can mislead readings

5. **Environmental Sensors**

- **Types:** Barometers (pressure), thermometers, hygrometers (humidity), and 61eider counters (radiation).
- **Purpose:** Establish environmental baselines and detect sudden deviations.
- **Integration:** Used in tandem with personal logs to verify claims of "uneasy feelings".

6. **Motion and Vibration Detectors**

- **Mechanism:** Infrared beam interruption, seismic sensors.
- **Use Case:** Detecting footsteps, object movements when no one is present.
- **Important:** Must be calibrated for location and ground stability.

7. **Spirit/Trigger Objects**

- **Definition:** Familiar or symbolic items placed to provoke interaction (e.g., toys, coins, religious artifacts).
- **Monitoring:** Often paired with video or motion sensors.
- **Scientific Skepticism:** Susceptible to environmental movement or suggestion bias.

9.4 Documentation and Recording Tools

Accurate documentation ensures that data is reliable, shareable, and reviewable. Common tools include:

- **Field Notebooks and Incident Logs:** Immediate manual recording of observations.
- **Voice Memos:** Quick annotations when writing is impractical.
- **Body-Worn Cameras:** Maintain investigator integrity during sensitive cases.
- **Timestamp Apps and Synchronizers:** Align all devices for cross-analysis.

Recommendation: Use redundant systems—e.g., two audio devices, independent cameras—to verify critical events.

9.5 Conceptual Tools and Methodologies

1. **Baseline Readings Protocol**

- **Purpose:** Establish natural environmental parameters before any investigation.
- **Includes:** EMF, temperature, humidity, light levels, sound levels.
- **Importance:** Prevents false positives and allows for data normalization.

2. **Interview and Testimonial Guidelines**

- **Structure:** Open-ended questions, cognitive interviewing techniques.
- **Caution:** Avoid leading questions or confirmation bias.
- **Documentation:** Record exact quotes; note nonverbal behavior.

3. **Hypothesis Development**

- **Structure:** Develop testable propositions for specific claims (e.g., "Apparitions appear near the attic when the temperature drops").
- **Frameworks:** Use null hypothesis to structure experiments.
- **Benefit:** Adds scientific discipline to fieldwork.

4. **Event Logging Templates**

- Include time, location, instruments involved, phenomena observed, and investigator commentary.
- Recommend use of shared spreadsheets or cloud-based apps for collaborative teams.

5. **Code of Ethics**

- Consent Protocols.
- Privacy and Data Security.
- Cultural and Religious Sensitivity.
- Psychological Risk Management.

9.6 Building a Mobile Kit

A mobile kit should be modular and adapted based on investigation type (indoor, outdoor, urban, rural). A basic mobile setup may include:

- **Primary Gear:** EMF meter, digital recorder, full-spectrum camera.
- **Support Gear:** Flashlights, backup batteries, lens wipes, tripods.
- **Safety Tools:** First aid kit, dust masks, gloves.
- **Logistical Tools:** Maps, walkie-talkies, legal permits (if required).

Packing Tip: Use foam-lined, waterproof cases. Keep equipment segmented by category.

9.7 Digital Tools and Software

1. **Audio Analysis Software**

- **Audacity, Adobe Audition, Wave Pad:** Used to filter, isolate, and analyze EVPs
- **Features:** Spectral analysis, noise reduction, equalization

2. **Image and Video Analysis**

- **Photoshop, Light room, Premiere Pro:** To adjust exposure and review anomalies frame-by-frame.
- **Scientific caution:** Enhancing images must never distort original integrity.

3. **Data Aggregation Platforms**

- Tools like Google Sheets or specialized paranormal logging apps.
- Enable cross-referencing of EMF, temperature, audio, and testimonial data.

4. **GIS and Mapping Tools**

- Used to analyze regional clusters of reports or phenomena.
- Useful in identifying ley lines, fault zones, or historically significant sites.

9.8 Team Tools and Communication Protocols

Internal Coordination:

- Shared team calendars and apps like Slack or Trello
- Clear role assignment: tech lead, interviewer, safety officer, documentation lead

In-Field Communication:

- Use hands-free radios or push-to-talk systems
- Night protocols: red-light flashlights, silent signals to minimize noise pollution

Post-Investigation Debriefing:

- Hold structured reviews after each case
- Use rubrics to evaluate success of instrumentation, safety, and data quality

9.9 Tool Limitations and Bias Awareness

It is vital to recognize the constraints and potential biases that tools may introduce:

- **False Positives:** Equipment may pick up non-paranormal anomalies.
- **Confirmation Bias:** Investigators may interpret data to fit expectations.
- **Technological Artifacts:** Software or hardware errors may distort data.
- **Human Factors:** Stress, fatigue, and darkness affect perception.

Mitigation requires peer review, triangulation (multiple tool validation), and rigorous documentation.

9.10 Instruments Used in Paranormal Investigations

1. **Environmental Sensing Equipment:**

- **EMF Meter (Electromagnetic Field Detector):** Detects fluctuations in electromagnetic fields.
- **Thermal Imaging Camera / Infrared Thermometer:** Detects heat signatures and cold spots.
- **Temperature Data Logger:** Records ongoing temperature changes.
- **Geophone / Vibration Sensor:** Detects minor floor vibrations.
- **Air Ion Counter:** Measures ion levels in the air.
- **Barometer / Pressure Sensor:** Measures atmospheric pressure changes.

2. **Audio Equipment**

- **Digital Voice Recorder (for EVP – Electronic Voice Phenomena):** Captures unexplained voices or noises.

- **Parabolic Microphone:** Enhances and records faint or distant sounds.
- **Spirit Box (or Ghost Box):** Scans radio frequencies to allow spirit voices.
- **Binaural Microphones:** Captures 3D audio for immersive analysis.

3. **Visual Recording Devices:**

- **Night Vision Cameras:** Captures images in low light conditions.
- **Full Spectrum Cameras:** Records in ultraviolet, visible, and infrared light.
- **Motion-Activated Cameras:** Automatically record when motion is detected.
- **360° Cameras:** Capture panoramic visuals.
- **Still Cameras:** Used for photographing anomalies.

4. **Communication Tools:**

- **Spirit Board / Ouija Board**: Traditional tool for communicating with spirits.
- **Dowsing Rods:** Believed to detect spiritual presence.
- **Pendulums:** Used for yes/no questions with spirits.
- **REM Pod:** Detects disturbances in electromagnetic fields.
- **SLS Camera:** Maps human-shaped figures using infrared light.

5. **Data Logging & Analysis Equipment:**

- **Digital Data Logger:** Records multiple environmental readings.
- **Laptop with Analysis Software:** For real-time or post-investigation analysis.
- **Software for Audio/Visual Analysis:** Enhances and examines captured data.

6. **Miscellaneous Tools**

- **Flashlights (red-light):** For safety and preserving night vision.
- **Walkie-Talkies:** For team communication.

- **Laser Grid Pen:** Projects a grid to detect disturbances.
- **Trigger Objects:** Items used to encourage spirit interaction.
- **Notepad or Mobile Apps:** For documentation.

9.11 Conclusion

An effective paranormal investigator must balance enthusiasm with critical thinking. The toolkit is not just a collection of gadgets but a manifestation of methodical discipline and ethical inquiry. Choosing and using tools responsibly allows for deeper insights, fewer errors, and greater public and academic trust in your work.

The next chapter will explore how to plan and conduct a full-scale investigation—bringing all these tools into action, from site research to debriefing.

Chapter Ten

Planning and Conducting a Field Investigation

10.1 Introduction

Field investigations represent the heart of practical paranormal research. A well-structured investigation integrates scientific method, logistical precision, ethical awareness, and interdisciplinary understanding. This chapter outlines a complete step-by-step framework—from site selection to post-investigation review—designed to enhance reliability and credibility in field investigations.

We explore planning strategies, team coordination, safety protocols, technical deployment, and post-investigation practices, all tailored for fieldwork in both residential and public spaces.

10.2 Pre-Investigation Preparation

A. Case Selection Criteria

Not every report warrants field deployment. Investigators must evaluate:

- Credibility of witnesses
- Consistency of reported phenomena
- Accessibility and legality of location
- Historical or environmental significance

Example Triage System:

- Anonymous, one time – Not Sufficient for System.
- Multiple witnesses, unclear data – Consider interview phase only.
- Verified history, ongoing events – Proceed to planning phase.

B. Research and Background Checks

Before stepping onto the site, comprehensive research should be conducted:

- Historical archives (property records, deaths, battles, ownership changes)

- Local folklore (newspaper archives, oral traditions)
- Geographical data (fault lines, mineral content, ley lines)
- Weather history (affects EMF readings and perceptions.

Use GIS software and public records to cross-check reports.

C. Permissions and Legalities

Obtain:

- Written consent from owners or authorities
- Insurance coverage for liability
- Waivers and NDAs signed by team and witnesses
- Local regulations regarding public land or religious sites

D. Preliminary Interviews

Interview residents or witnesses before the investigation:

- Document mental/emotional state
- Avoid leading questions
- Record exact times, sounds, smells, visual descriptions
- Clarify triggers (certain rooms, times, objects)

10.3 Planning the Investigation

A. Defining Objectives

Clearly outline:

- What are you trying to detect? (EVP, apparitions, temperature shifts)
- What tools will be used?
- What will validate or refute the claims?

Example Objective:

"To verify claims of footsteps in the attic using directional audio recorders and vibration sensors between 22:00 and 01:00 over two consecutive nights."

B. Team Assignments

Assign roles with redundancy in mind:

- Lead Investigator
- Technical Lead
- Documentation Officer
- Witness Liaison
- Safety/First Aid Officer
- Skeptical Analyst

Use communication apps or earpieces for in-field updates.

C. Site Walkthrough and Equipment Mapping

Conduct a daylight walkthrough:

- Identify hotspots, EMF baselines, and environmental hazards
- Place discreet markers for sensor deployment
- Sketch floor plans or use LIDAR mapping apps

D. Equipment Checklist

Ensure all equipment is:

- Calibrated and tested
- Time-synchronized
- Battery-backed
- Weather-proofed (for outdoor)

Include backup gear, headlamps, data storage, and protective cases.

10.4 Conducting the Investigation

A. Entry Protocol

- Begin with team briefing and opening log entries
- Use protection rituals if desired (investigators should not impose religious acts on others)
- Silence non-essential electronics
- Note current weather, environmental readings, and noise levels

B. Surveillance Setup

Position devices at:

- Reported phenomenon hotspots
- Entrances/exits to monitor unauthorized interference
- Power sources (with surge protectors)
- Hidden trigger objects (monitored by motion sensors)

Ensure:

- Devices are labeled and tamper-sealed
- Redundancy: e.g., two cameras covering same zone from different angles

C. Active Investigation Phases

Split sessions into:

- Silent Observation (20–30 mins): Baseline monitoring
- Interactive Sessions: Asking questions, using spirit boxes, using trigger objects
- Roving Patrols: Unscripted movement and surveillance

Time-stamp every action for cross-referencing during analysis.

D. Incident Logging

Use incident report templates for each occurrence:

- Time/date
- Observer's name
- Equipment active
- Environmental conditions
- Objective description (no interpretations during logging)

Assign someone to log potential psychological effects (dizziness, disorientation) in team members.

E. Safety and Emergency Readiness

Always keep:

- First-aid kits
- Fire extinguishers (especially in abandoned sites)
- Maps and emergency exit plans

- A team exit protocol for extreme phenomena or health risks

Avoid:

- Solo investigation
- Climbing unstable structures
- Performing rituals without consent or clarity

10.5 Post-Investigation Procedure

A. Securing Data

Immediately after the investigation:

- Back up data on at least two separate drives
- Label files by time, location, and device
- Store raw footage unaltered (required for peer review)

B. Preliminary Team Debrief

Hold same-day debrief:

- Discuss major observations
- Note gaps in coverage or technical failures
- Record subjective impressions for contextual understanding

C. Data Review and Analysis

Within 3–7 days, conduct systematic review:

- **Audio/EVP analysis:** Spectral visualization, volume normalization
- **Video review:** Frame-by-frame with timestamp cross-reference
- **Sensor logs:** Correlate EMF or motion spikes with other phenomena

Involve at least one skeptical reviewer to challenge assumptions.

D. Report Compilation

Structure the final report with the following components:

1. Executive Summary
2. Background Research
3. Investigation Objectives
4. Methodology

5. Findings (with multimedia samples)
6. Interpretation and Limitations
7. Ethical Compliance Summary
8. Conclusion and Recommendations

Include annotated photos and sensor logs as appendices.

E. Follow-Up

Contact witnesses and property owners with:

- Summary of findings
- Recommendations for spiritual support or psychological evaluation (if needed)
- Referrals (to clergy, counselors, parapsychologists)

Ensure emotional closure is supported—especially if trauma was reported.

10.6 Common Challenges in Field Investigation

- Power Loss - Batteri–s drained without cause
- Data Corruption - Audio/Video files fail
- Equipment Interface – Wi-Fi, Phone towers cause false reading
- Witness Retraction – Client withdraw permission post-fact
- Anecdotal Reasoning – Accepting personal stories as evidence
- Equipment Fallacy – Trusting devices without understanding them
- Emotional Bias – Letting fear or excitement dictate conclusions.

10.7 Conclusion

A well-executed field investigation is a synthesis of scientific process, human psychology, technological skill, and logistical precision. Planning is as crucial as execution. When conducted responsibly and rigorously, a field investigation not only reveals potential paranormal phenomena but also upholds credibility and respect within the broader scientific and public spheres.

Chapter Eleven

Analyzing and Interpreting Collected Data

11.1 Introduction

Data collection in the field is only the first half of the investigative process. The true value of a paranormal investigation emerges through critical, structured analysis of that data. Unlike anecdotal storytelling, which may emphasize emotion or belief, analysis in this discipline must strive for objectivity, clarity, reproducibility, and transparency.

This chapter focuses on post-investigation data processing, categorization, correlation, and interpretation using both qualitative and quantitative approaches. We will also address common biases, error correction, and the ethical use of subjective experiences.

11.2 Types of Data Collected

Investigators often handle several forms of data, including:

A. **Audio Data**

- EVP recordings (electronic voice phenomena).
- Ambient sounds and anomalies.
- Microphone interference or distortions.

B. **Visual Data**

- Infrared footage
- Night-vision and thermal imaging
- Photographic anomalies (orbs, shadows, apparitions)

C. **Sensor Data**

- EMF readings (fluctuation patterns)
- Temperature changes
- Motion sensor triggers
- Vibration or pressure pad activations

D. **Observational Logs**

- Investigator notes

- Time-stamped journal entries
- Witness descriptions

11.3 Initial Data Processing

A. Data Integrity Measures

- **Create backups:** Before opening or editing any file
- **Checksum verification:** To detect corrupted files
- **Metadata preservation:** Avoid re-saving files in a way that modifies timestamps

B. Labeling and Organizing

Standardize file names:

- Keep file name as simples and clear as possible with client/property name with reference number and date of investigation done.

Use folders such as:

- Audio Raw
- Video Processed
- Sensor Logs
- Analysis Notes
- Redacted for Public Sharing

11.4 Audio Analysis (EVP and Sound Events)

A. Tools Used

- Audacity, Adobe Audition, Audeme EVP Software
- Spectrogram viewers (e.g., Sonic Visualiser)
- Noise reduction and waveform smoothing

B. Procedure

- Import recordings and normalize volume
- Apply noise filters to isolate potential voices
- Use spectrogram to identify anomalies
- Tag and extract potential EVPs
- Review anomalies in team without priming (avoid "suggesting" what it sounds like).

C. Interpretation Criteria

- **Class A EVP:** Clear, intelligible, reproducible
- **Class B EVP:** Distorted but understandable
- **Class C EVP:** Unclear or subjective

Use peer review panels or blind listening to verify credibility.

11.5 Video and Photographic Analysis

A. Visual Anomaly Checklist

- Light source and angle?
- Dust or insects in motion?
- Lens flare or digital noise?
- Reflections or shadows?
- Infrared bounce artifacts?

B. Software Tools

- Adobe Premiere, DaVinci Resolve, VLC
- Deep frame-by-frame viewing (24–60 fps)
- Image editing software for exposure, contrast testing

C. Thermal or Night Vision Footage

- Compare anomalies to temperature logs
- Check for human or animal heat signatures
- Eliminate mechanical/electrical interference

11.6 Sensor Data Interpretation

A. EMF Pattern Recognition

Look for:

- Spikes correlating with reported events
- Baseline fluctuations
- Sustained high readings in locations with no electronics

Graph readings over time and compare against:

- Motion sensor triggers
- Temperature drops
- Audio anomalies

B. Temperature Drops

Criteria:

- Sudden vs gradual drops
- Duration (temporary vs sustained)
- Indoor vs outdoor impact
- Time correlation with other phenomena

Use environmental controls (like HVAC logs) to rule out mechanical causes.

11.7 Qualitative Analysis: Observational Data

A. Content Coding of Investigator Notes

Identify:

- Recurrent descriptions (e.g., "pressure on chest," "cold breath")
- Shared impressions between different investigators
- Subjective feelings vs observable phenomena

Use coding techniques:

- Code A: Emotional response
- Code B: Physical sensation
- Code C: Visual/Audio anomaly
- Code D: Equipment interference

This method helps turn subjective logs into systematized patterns.

B. Witness Testimony Analysis

Cross-reference:

- Witness narratives with logged times
- Descriptive overlap with team journals
- Visual/audio data supporting testimony

Note any psychological influences (grief, sleep disorder, suggestion) that may shape testimony.

11.8 Cross-Modality Correlation

The strongest evidence comes from multiple data sources aligning in time and effect.

Case Example:

- EVP voice recorded at 01:16
- Simultaneous EMF spike
- Thermal camera shows shadow movement
- Motion sensor triggered

When four data points converge, the event holds greater investigative weight—though never absolute proof.

11.9 Avoiding Bias in Interpretation

A. Confirmation Bias

Avoid analyzing with the intent to "find the ghost." Remain open to both paranormal and mundane explanations.

B. Pareidolia

Human tendency to see patterns (like faces or voices) where none exist. Use multiple reviewers to validate findings.

C. Groupthink

Team consensus may pressure individuals to agree with majority views. Blind reviewing can reduce this risk.

11.10 Reporting Findings Ethically

A. Transparency

Include:

- Description of tools used
- Dates/times of data capture
- Known malfunctions or anomalies

B. Avoid Overstating

Instead of:

"This clearly proves the presence of a spirit,"

Say:

"A recorded voice-like anomaly aligns with reported activity. No current environmental cause has been identified."

C. Use Clear Labels

- Unexplained anomaly (not "ghost")
- Environmental deviation (not "haunting")

D. Preserve Privacy

If clients are involved, redact:

- Names
- Addresses
- Sensitive emotional or mental health data

11.11 Summary

Data interpretation in paranormal investigation is both an art and a science. By combining technical analysis with critical reasoning and ethical caution, investigators can separate compelling evidence from false positives, and potentially uncover patterns worthy of further exploration.

The strength of any case lies not in the drama of the encounter, but in the rigor of the analysis that follows it.

Chapter Twelve

Skepticism, Hoaxes and Debunking

12.1 Introduction

Skepticism is not the enemy of paranormal investigation—it is its intellectual backbone. Without healthy doubt, investigations risk devolving into confirmation-seeking ventures rather than critical explorations of anomalous phenomena.

This chapter explores the constructive role of skepticism, the prevalence and mechanics of hoaxes, and the systematic process of debunking. Rather than dismissing all claims, skepticism insists on methodological integrity, replicability, and plausible alternatives before attributing an experience to the paranormal.

12.2 The Role of Skepticism in Paranormal Studies

A. Scientific Skepticism vs. Cynicism

- **Skepticism:** Demands strong evidence before accepting extraordinary claims. Rooted in inquiry.
- **Cynicism:** Rejects claims outright, often without engagement.

A disciplined investigator welcomes skepticism as it protects against intellectual error and maintains public credibility.

B. Philosophy of Falsifiability

According to philosopher Karl Popper, a claim is scientific only if it can be falsified. In paranormal research:

- A theory must allow for disproof.
- Claims like "ghosts exist, but hide from science" are non-falsifiable and scientifically meaningless.

Thus, even if absolute proof is elusive, your methodology must be disprovable to be credible.

12.3 Common Types of Hoaxes

Intentional deception is more common in paranormal cases than many realize. Motivations range from attention-seeking to financial gain.

A. Hoaxes by Witnesses

- Fabricated EVP recordings
- Staged poltergeist activity
- Fake photos using double exposure or mobile apps

B. Property Owner Hoaxes

- Claims exaggerated to increase tourism or media attention
- False "haunted" claims for property value or thematic branding

C. Digital and AI-Based Hoaxes

- Deep fake videos
- AI-generated spirit images
- Voice-cloned EVPs

Investigators must now vet not only analog tricks, but also sophisticated digital fakes.

12.4 Warning Signs of a Hoax

- Over Dramatic Story telling – Witness changes story frequently or embellishes events
- Equipment always works "Too Well" – Unnatural consistency in capturing Phenomena.
- Financial Incentive – Tickets, media rights or merchandise offered.
- Evidence Appears After Group Leaves – Images or sound mysteriously "found" later by the client.
- Witness Control Access – Limits to where or when investigators can observe.

12.5 Debunking: Methodical Elimination of Natural Causes

Debunking does not mean denying all phenomena. It means testing for natural or man-made explanations before assigning paranormal labels.

A. Environmental Factors

- Drafts → Slamming doors or cold spots

- Old plumbing → Banging sounds mistaken for knocks
- Mold exposure → Visual or auditory hallucinations
- Electromagnetic hypersensitivity → Causing paranoia, nausea, or hallucinations

B. Technological Interference

- Radio signals → May be picked up by poorly shielded speakers
- Wi-Fi routers → Cause interference on EMF detectors
- Infrared bounce → Reflecting back into night vision cameras
- Smart devices → Auto-triggers mimicking spirit activity

C. Human Psychology

- Infrasound (low-frequency sound): Can induce dread or visual distortions
- Sleep paralysis: Misinterpreted as paranormal attack
- Pareidolia: Seeing faces or figures in shadows, static, etc.

12.6 Debunking Procedure

- **Baseline Readings:** Capture EMF, temperature, and ambient light/sound levels when no activity is present.
- **Environmental Testing:** Recreate claims under different conditions.
- **Equipment Cross-Validation:** Use multiple brands or analog backups.
- **Consult Experts:** Plumbers, electricians, HVAC technicians, and even psychologists.
- **Blind Test Witnesses:** Without prompting, ask them to describe activity in "hot spots" to test for suggestion.

Case Example: "Phantom Footsteps"

Claim: Footsteps heard nightly in an abandoned mansion.

Debunking Steps:

- EMF stable.
- Sound recorded matched rats in attic confirmed by exterminator.
- Infrared camera showed nesting sites.
- Residents' anxiety explained through infrasound from HVAC system.

Conclusion: No paranormal activity. Misinterpretation of mundane factors.

12.7 Maintaining Objectivity Under-Pressure

Even experienced teams can feel compelled to "find something." This pressure—internal or client-driven—can undermine objectivity.

- **Best Practice:** If nothing is found, report that result honestly.
- **Avoid:** Dramatizing mild findings for public interest.
- **Peer:** Review your findings with uninvolved third parties.

12.8 The Ethical Value of Debunking

Debunking is not just about disproving—it:

- Protects clients from fear or exploitation
- Upholds investigative integrity
- Improves public trust in the field
- Encourages critical thinking and scientific respectability

12.9 Summary

A paranormal investigator's greatest strength is not a device or belief—it is disciplined skepticism. By embracing falsifiability, identifying hoaxes, understanding human perception, and eliminating natural causes before jumping to conclusions, investigators preserve the field's intellectual dignity.

Paranormal phenomena, if they exist, will withstand skeptical scrutiny. In fact, only when they do can they ever be taken seriously.

Chapter Thirteen

Ethics, Consent and Client Relationships

13.1 Introduction

Paranormal investigations often intersect with deeply personal, emotional, and psychological experiences. Unlike conventional scientific research, this field requires frequent interaction with clients who are distressed, vulnerable, or even mentally unwell.

For that reason, ethical conduct in paranormal investigations is non-negotiable. This chapter outlines core principles such as informed consent, privacy protection, mental health awareness, and responsible disclosure of findings. Ethics is not only a matter of professionalism—it is the foundation of public trust in the field.

13.2 The Importance of Ethics in Paranormal Investigation

A. Why It Matters

- Paranormal claims often arise from stress, grief, trauma, or fear
- Investigators may be perceived as authorities or spiritual advisors
- Mis-steps can lead to emotional harm, reputational damage, or legal consequences

B. Core Ethical Values

- Respect: For clients, property, and the unknown
- Transparency: Honest communication at every stage
- Non-maleficence: "First, do no harm"
- Objectivity: Avoid imposing your beliefs or assumptions

13.3 Informed Consent and Client Communication

A. What is Informed Consent?

Informed consent means clients:

1. Fully understand what the investigation involves
2. Are aware of risks and limitations

3. Voluntarily agree without coercion

B. Consent Form Should Include:

- Description of the investigation process
- Duration and time of visits
- Types of equipment used
- Audio/video recording terms
- Privacy and data handling policy
- Withdrawal rights at any stage

C. When to Avoid Investigations:

- Minors present without parental consent
- Mental health issues appear unaddressed
- Hostility, conflict, or instability in the environment

13.4 Privacy and Confidentiality

A. Client Data Security

- Keep all digital files (audio, video, logs) encrypted.
- Use secure storage platforms with limited access.
- Avoid storing data on personal or unprotected devices.

B. Anonymity in Publications

If you intend to share results or publish:

- Use aliases or initials.
- Mask identifiable features in media.
- Obtain explicit media release forms.

C. Respecting Property

- Do not explore unauthorized areas.
- Avoid touching personal items.
- Leave no physical trace of your visit.

13.5 Managing Client Expectations

A. Avoiding Overpromising

Do not claim to:

- "Remove spirits" unless properly trained in spiritual practices
- Guarantee activity will stop

- Provide final proof of the afterlife

B. Setting Boundaries

- Make clear you are investigators, not therapists or clergy
- Establish contact limits after case completion
- Discourage dependency on your team for emotional support

C. Crisis Situations

If a client shows signs of emotional breakdown, hallucination, or suicidal ideation, pause the investigation and recommend professional mental health assistance.

13.6 Cultural and Religious Sensitivity

A. Respect Belief Systems

Clients may interpret experiences through:

- Christian, Hindu, Islamic, Buddhist, or Indigenous frameworks
- Folk traditions (e.g., djinns, curses, karmic hauntings)

Avoid mocking or invalidating these perspectives, even if your methods are secular.

B. Involving Spiritual Advisors

If requested by the client:

- Work collaboratively with priests, shamans, monks, or imams
- Do not override religious rites with scientific protocols

13.7 Working with Vulnerable Populations

A. Children

- Never conduct investigations with or around minors without parental/guardian supervision
- Avoid discussing frightening events or interpretations
- Use child psychologists when necessary

B. Elderly

- Be gentle with questions
- Ensure full clarity before any data collection
- Watch for signs of confusion, dementia, or exploitation

C. Grieving Individuals

- Avoid suggesting that deceased loved ones are "present"

- Be cautious in interpreting EVPs or shadows as messages
- Recommend bereavement counseling where appropriate

13.8 Post-Investigation Ethics

A. Disclosure of Findings

- Present results factually, without exaggeration
- Allow clients to ask questions
- Emphasize that no conclusion is 100% definitive

B. Follow-Up

- Offer a final debrief or summary report.
- Avoid repeated visits unless justified by evidence.
- Refer clients to spiritual support or therapy, not more paranormal groups, unless necessary.

C. Case Closure

- Respect a client's decision to end contact.
- Do not reuse the property or case details for future media without consent.
- Consider sending a closure letter summarizing your findings and thanking them.

13.9 Avoiding Exploitation in Media and Publicity

A. Reality TV and YouTube Culture

- Avoid sensationalizing suffering for views or funding.
- Never film clients without informed, signed consent.
- Do not stage evidence to attract attention.

B. Professional Boundaries

- Maintain professional tone in all public commentary.
- Avoid posting during emotionally sensitive stages of the investigation.
- Don't "name and shame" debunked clients.

13.10 Ethical Case Example

Case: "The Crying Widow"

A client, recently widowed, reports nightly weeping sounds.

Investigation shows:

- No EMF anomalies
- Sound traced to water pipes
- Client reveals auditory grief hallucinations

Action Taken:

- Recommended grief counseling
- Provided full report
- Declined to label experience as paranormal

This case demonstrates ethical restraint, client protection, and responsible practice.

13.11 Summary

In the pursuit of the paranormal, your credibility depends not only on evidence, but on how you treat people. Ethical practice ensures:

- Your work is trusted
- Clients are respected
- Findings are handled with maturity and professionalism

Ultimately, an ethical investigator acts with integrity, compassion, and discipline, recognizing that the unknown may be far less dangerous than the harm caused by unethical behavior.

Chapter Fourteen

How to Set Up Your Paranormal Investigation Team

14.1 Introduction

Establishing a well-structured paranormal investigation team is essential for conducting ethical, methodical, and evidence-based inquiries into anomalous phenomena. While passion may initiate interest in the field, only a cohesive, trained, and professional team can ensure credibility and long-term success.

This chapter outlines the steps and best practices for creating and managing a paranormal investigation team, including considerations for team composition, training, ethics, logistics, and internal communication.

14.2 Define Your Team's Mission and Scope

Before recruiting members, establish a clear mission statement and operational scope:

Sample Mission Statement:

"To document, analyze, and research unexplained phenomena using scientific principles and ethical practices, with respect for client confidentiality and cultural beliefs."

Scope of Operations May Include:

- Private home investigations
- Historical site studies
- Urban legends and folklore explorations
- EVP or photographic research
- Educational workshops or public outreach

Clarity of purpose will influence recruitment, training, and funding decisions.

14.3 Core Roles and Responsibilities

A. Team Leader / Case Manager

- Coordinates investigations
- Liaises with clients
- Reviews reports and evidence
- Makes final calls on team actions

B. Technical Specialist

- Handles equipment (EMF meters, thermal cameras, recorders)
- Maintains logs and calibrates tools
- Manages digital storage and backups

C. Researcher / Historian

- Investigates location history
- Gathers client background
- Cross-references with folklore, archived materials, or newspaper records

D. Psychological Observer / Interviewer

- Conducts pre-visit interviews
- Assesses psychological well-being of witnesses or clients
- Screens for mental health red flags (non-clinical)

E. Data Analyst

- Reviews audio, video, and photographic data post-investigation
- Organizes and compiles potential anomalies
- Filters out false positives

F. Ethics Officer / Debrief Coordinator

- Ensures consent is documented
- Enforces ethical guidelines
- Leads team debriefs and psychological aftercare

G. Media & Documentation Specialist (optional)

- Manages case reports and visual materials
- Handles online presence (if applicable)
- Documents procedures for future training

Note: Smaller teams may have members performing multiple roles. Flexibility is key.

14.4 Recruitment and Vetting

Qualities to Look For:

- Integrity, discretion, and professionalism
- Open-minded skepticism
- Teamwork and emotional intelligence
- Basic understanding of investigative or scientific methods
- Respect for cultural, spiritual, and personal boundaries

Where to Find Members:

- Academic or paranormal forums
- Local colleges (psychology, history, media programs)
- Science clubs or amateur research groups
- Community volunteer networks

Vetting Includes:

- Background checks (especially when working in private homes)
- Reference checks
- Observational probation period

14.5 Internal Training and Skill Development

Create a training curriculum for new members, which may include:

- Paranormal Phenomena – Categories, Case studies & Misconceptions.
- Equipment Handling – Safe & accurate use of tools.
- Ethics – Consent, privacy & cultural sensitivity.

14.6 Communication Protocols and Chain of Command

Establish consistent and secure internal communication:

- Use encrypted platforms (e.g., Signal, ProtonMail) for sensitive data
- Maintain digital logs of each investigation
- Clarify who speaks to clients, media, or property owners
- Set up emergency contact plans during high-risk investigations (e.g., abandoned buildings, night visits)

Clear hierarchy ensures smooth, conflict-free operations.

14.7 Equipment Acquisition and Management

A. Essential Starter Equipment:

- EMF Meter (Trifield or K-II)
- Digital voice recorder (for EVPs)
- Thermometer (laser or digital probe)
- Infrared or full-spectrum camera.
- Tripods, lighting, batteries, and extension cords.
- Notebook or data log sheets.

B. Storage and Inventory Tips:

- Assign gear to specific members.
- Conduct monthly functionality checks.
- Track purchases and replacements in shared inventory sheets.
-

For ethical and safety reasons, avoid using fake or gimmicky tools.

14.8 Community Building and Outreach

Promote transparency and public education:

- Host community Q&As or history talks
- Attend or speak at conventions and conferences
- Publish anonymized case studies in newsletters or academic journals
- Collaborate with local historians, cultural groups, or scientists

Community trust increases case access and reduces stigma.

14.9 Sustaining Team Morale and Cohesion

Running a paranormal team is emotionally demanding. To avoid burnout:

- Schedule debriefs after intense cases
- Rotate roles to prevent overwork
- Encourage open feedback and peer mentorship
- Celebrate team milestones
- Address conflict early with impartial mediation

A successful team is not just functional, but emotionally resilient.

14.10 Funding your Team

Startup costs are moderate, but sustainability requires planning

- Members Contribution.
- Donation / Crowd-funding.
- Public Lectures / Workshops.
- Merchandise (Shirts, Books).
- Partnering with Institutions.

Always try to do this avoid charging client for paranormal investigation – it may damage the reputation.

14.11 Team Structure with Responsibility

- Director – Oversees operations & case selection.
- Lead Investigator – Co-ordinates field work & evidence review.
- Technical Head – Manages gear & data integrity.
- Research Officer – Gathers historical and social context.
- Ethics liaison Officer – Handles Consent, culture respect and safety.

14.12 Conclusion

Setting up a paranormal investigation team is a multidimensional process requiring both structure and sensitivity. It involves recruiting ethical, open-minded individuals, providing rigorous training, and maintaining a culture of respect, transparency, and intellectual honesty.

With a strong foundation, your team can contribute meaningfully to the field—whether through research, education, or service to those experiencing unexplained events.

14.13 Sample Client Intake Form

Paranormal Investigation Client Intake & Consent Form

Date of Request: ____________________

Case ID: ____________________

Investigator Assigned: ____________________

A. Client Information

- Full Name: ______________________________________

- Address of Property: ____________________________
- Phone Number: ________________________________
- Email: ______________________________________
- Preferred Contact Method: ☐ Phone ☐ Email ☐ Other

B. Description of Reported Activity

1. Describe the phenomena you've experienced:
2. How long has this been occurring?

☐ Less than a week
☐ 1–3 weeks
☐ 1–6 months
☐ Over 6 months

3. Any recent emotional trauma or renovations in the location?

☐ Yes ☐ No

If yes, please describe: __________________________________

4. Have you or anyone else been physically harmed or felt threatened?

☐ Yes ☐ No

5. Have any religious, spiritual, or professional services already been consulted?

☐ Yes ☐ No

If yes, specify: ____

C. Consent and Liability

☐ I understand that this is a non-scientific, non-religious investigation conducted for documentation and research purposes.

☐ I authorize the investigation team to conduct audio, video, and environmental recordings on the premises.

☐ I understand the team will not remove or exorcise any entity, nor make any medical or psychological diagnosis.

☐ I release the team from liability for unforeseen emotional or spiritual experiences.

Client Signature: ____________________

Date: ____________________

----

2. Code of Ethics for Paranormal Teams

Core Principles

1. Respect and Confidentiality

• Treat all clients, witnesses, and team members with respect.

• Protect the privacy of all case-related information.

2. Scientific Neutrality

• Remain objective in data collection.

• Never fabricate or alter evidence.

3. Cultural Sensitivity

• Acknowledge and respect spiritual and cultural practices of clients.

• Refrain from imposing personal beliefs.

4. Informed Consent

• Secure written permission for all investigations.

• Clarify the limits and purpose of the investigation before beginning.

5. Safety and Legality

• Never trespass or investigate without owner consent.

• Always prioritize physical and emotional safety.

6. Transparency and Accountability

• Keep clear records of findings and decisions.

• Address complaints or internal misconduct promptly.

Ethical Violations May Lead To:

• Immediate dismissal from the team

• Revocation of investigation privileges

• Reporting to appropriate authorities (if applicable)

All members must sign and abide by this code.

3. Sample Team Charter / Mission Document

Paranormal Inquiry and Documentation Team (PIDT) Charter

Mission Statement

We seek to explore and document unexplained phenomena through ethical, research-oriented investigations grounded in scientific reasoning and cultural respect.

Team Objectives

- Provide free, confidential investigations for individuals or communities reporting paranormal activity.
- Train members in scientific method, ethics, and technical equipment use.
- Promote education on critical thinking, folklore, and paranormal history.
- Contribute findings to public or academic databases with consent.

Meetings and Operations

- Monthly team meetings (virtual or in-person)
- Minimum one training drill per quarter
- Written reports due within 10 days of investigation

Membership

- All members agree to uphold the Code of Ethics
- Probationary period: 3 months
- Dismissal may result from ethical or legal violations